Writing Lessons from the Front: Book 1

The Plot Skeleton

*a practical, bare-bones approach
to plotting your story*

Angela Hunt

A condensed version of this booklet was first published in *A Novel Idea* (Tyndale House), a collection of useful tips and techniques for novelists.

Book 1 in the *Writing Lessons from the Front* Series

Hunt Haven
Press

Visit Angela Hunt's Web site at www.angelahuntbooks.com

ISBN:0615834086
ISBN-13: 978-0615834085

DEDICATION

To all the teachers who ever scribbled my pages
with a red pen: thank you.

1 THE ONE AND ONLY CHAPTER

When we were in school, our English teachers gave us explicit details about how to write a five-paragraph theme: introduction, thesis sentence, point one, point two, point three, and conclusion. But when it came to writing creative fiction, odds are that your teacher said, "Just tell me a story."

No wonder so many storytellers falter when it comes to creating their own stories! We move from the ordered world of nonfiction into a world which can appear to be a whirling ebb and flow of ideas. To the uninitiated, it can feel like a riptide and it's hard to make any headway.

But creative fiction does have a structure, and it's been around for ages. From Joseph Campbell's study of the hero's journey to Syd Field's exploration of screenwriting structure, others have found and analyzed plot structure with sometimes confusing terms.

A few years ago, I was hired to teach writing to homeschooled students from third through twelfth grades. I wanted to teach them to plot, so I searched for a method that was easy to understand and yet completely sound. After studying several plotting techniques and boiling them down to their basic elements, I developed what I call the plot skeleton. It combines the spontaneity of "seat of the pants" writing with the discipline of an outline. It requires a writer to know where he's going, but it leaves room for the joy of discovery on the journey.

Best of all, the method is visual. You don't have to have a lick of artistic ability, but if you can draw a round head, some ribs, and some skinny leg bones, you can draw a skeleton that will guide you through the plotting process.

A Bare Bones Outline

Imagine, if you will, that you and I are sitting in a room with one hundred other writers. If you were to ask each person to describe their plotting process, you'd probably get a hundred different answers. Writers' methods vary according to their personalities and we are all different. Mentally. Emotionally. Physically.

If, however, those one hundred writers were to pass behind an x-ray machine, you'd discover that except for slight gender differences we all possess remarkably similar skeletons. Unless someone has been unfortunate enough to experience some kind of deformity, beneath our disguising skin, hair, and clothing, our skeletons would nearly indistinguishable.

In the same way, though writers vary in their methods, good stories are composed of remarkably similar skeletons. Stories with "good bones" can be found in picture books and movies, plays and films. The only difference in most stories is length, and length is usually determined by the breadth of the work—how many subplots are involved, and how many complications the protagonist must face.

Many fine writers carefully outline their plots before they begin the first chapter while others describe themselves as "seat of the pants" plotters. But when the story is finished, a seat-of-the-pants novel will usually contain the same elements as a carefully-plotted book. Why? Because whether you plan from the beginning or work through intuition, novels need structure to support the story.

When I sit down to plan a new book, the first thing I do is sketch my smiling little skeleton.

To illustrate the plot skeleton in this article, I'm going to refer frequently to *The Wizard of Oz*, *The Sound of Music*, and a lovely foreign film you may have never seen, *Mostly Martha*.

One more thing: my lessons are never intended to be a set of rules that must never be broken. What I want to offer are guides to the art of writing. Take what you learn here, visualize it, practice it, and then use it in your own way to create your story.

The Skull

The skull represents the main character, the protagonist. A lot of beginning novelists have a hard time deciding who the main character is, so settle that question right away. Even in an ensemble cast, one character should be more predominant than the others. Your reader wants to place himself into your story world, and it's helpful if you can give him a sympathetic character with whom he or she can relate. Ask yourself, "Whose story is this?" That is your protagonist.

At the very beginning of your story, this main character should be dealing with two situations, which I represent in the skeleton by two yawning eye sockets: one obvious problem, one hidden need. Here's a tip: hidden needs, which usually involve basic human emotions, are usually resolved or met by the end of the story. They are at the center of the protagonist's "inner journey," or character change, while the "outer journey" is concerned with the main events of the plot. Hidden needs often arise from wounds in a character's past.

Consider *The Wizard of Oz*. At the beginning of the film, Dorothy needs to save her dog from Miss Gulch, who has arrived at the farm to take Toto because he bit Miss Gulch's scrawny leg— a straightforward and obvious problem. Dorothy's *hidden* need is depicted but not directly emphasized when she stands by the pigpen and sings "Somewhere Over the Rainbow." Do children live with Uncle Henry and Aunt Em if all is fine with Mom and Dad? No. Though we are not told what happened to Dorothy's parents, it's clear that something has splintered her family and Dorothy's unhappy about the result. Her hidden need, the object of her inner journey, is to accept her new home.

The Sound of Music opens with young Maria dancing and singing in a mountain meadow. As we watch, we learn that this free spirited woman loves music and life, and that she has voluntarily entered a convent—to serve God and others, we may safely assume. But the girl, dear as she is, is simply not fitting in. The other nuns love her, but she distracts them from their prayers and she can't seem to keep her lively spirit from showing up at times when she should be quiet and contemplative. The nuns sing, "How Do you Solve A Problem Like Maria?" Like the song says, molding Maria to convent life is like holding a moonbeam in your hand— impossible. A fairly obvious problem.

Maria's hidden need is the very urge that brought her to the convent. She has a need to love God and serve others, and that's what she's trying—not very successfully—to do at the convent.

Mostly Martha opens with the title character lying on her therapist's couch and talking about all that is required to cook the perfect pigeon. Since she's in a therapist's office, we assume she has a problem, and the therapist addresses this directly: "Martha, why are you here?"

"Because," she answers, "my boss will fire me if I don't go to therapy."

Ah—her obvious problem involves her work and her boss. Immediately we also know that Martha is high-strung. She wears her hair tightly wound into a bun and is precise and politely controlling in her kitchen. This woman lives for food, but though she assures us in a voiceover that all a cook needs for a perfectly lovely dinner is "fish and sauce," we see her venture downstairs to ask her new neighbor if he'd like to join her for dinner. He can't, but we clearly see that Martha needs company. She needs people in her life. Like all of us, she needs love and companionship.

So—as you consider the story you're writing, have you settled on one protagonist? There will be other characters, of course, but have you found the one character who will change the most? The person the reader can "inhabit" for the length of the story? This should probably be the character who undergoes the greatest change over the course of your story.

Now, have you opened *in media res*, or in the middle of the action? You don't have to open your story with a bomb blast or a kidnapping, but you should open in the middle of an interesting problem—the protagonist is rushing to meet someone and has a flat tire, or she's trying to cook the perfect dinner and burns the entrée. Let us see this character up to his neck in ordinary life, and let us see how he handles stress. Let us hear what his neighbors think of him. Let us watch him grapple with an interesting problem, and then, through subtext, action, and reaction, let us see the hidden need in his life. Don't explain it, just reveal it by letting us observe him in his ordinary world.

Before we leave this development of the protagonist—and you may need up to 20 or 25 percent of the book to paint a complete picture—add a little smile to that face on your skeleton. Let it remind you that the reader needs to see something admirable in your protagonist.

Maybe she keeps her chin up when she loses her job; maybe he can remain calm when everyone else panics. Maybe she's a single mother who gives up dinner with a handsome man in order to help her son with his homework. Maybe he's a judge who refuses a bribe offered by a Mafia messenger . . . at great personal risk.

We admire Dorothy because she's loyal to her dog, she's plucky, and she's brave enough to run away from home, then compassionate enough to return when she realizes that Auntie Em might worry about her.

We admire Maria from the convent because she is a free spirit, because the nuns love her, and because she's so *good*. She's pretty, and she sings, so what's not to love?

We admire Martha the chef because she's a true artist, and exceptionally good at her job. We nearly always admire those who have reached the top of their craft because we know it takes skill and hard work to achieve that kind of success. So we admire Martha for knowing how to cook a pigeon . . . and then we sympathize with her when she can't find someone to share her elegant dinner.

Even if your protagonist is what would traditionally be considered a bad guy, let us see *something* in him that's admirable. *The Godfather's* Don Corleone was the godfather of a major crime syndicate, but the Don and his family had a set of ethics. Yes, they killed people, but they drew the line at selling drugs because they didn't want to harm children.

Though he wasn't the protagonist of the *Silence of the Lambs*, Hannibal Lecter was a sadistic serial killer and cannibal, yet he was so clever and intelligent that some part of us couldn't help but admire how he managed to outsmart the slimy prison warden. And we certainly rooted for Clarice, the wounded F.B.I. trainee who was trying to find a serial murderer.

We want to admire the protagonist; we yearn to feel sympathy and understanding for him. Because once we develop a solid affinity for him, we'll stick around when the real action begins.

Take a good look at your protagonist—from what you've written thus far, will the reader find him admirable? Can you make him really, really good at what he does? Can you give him a vulnerability, a real soft spot for his child, his dog, his wife? Can you take a moment to show us that he has strong character and a sense of morals? Can you display his sense of humor? We always admire people who can keep smiling in the midst of turmoil.

And the head bone's connected to the neck bone . . .

Usually the first few chapters of a novel are involved with the business of establishing the protagonist in a specific time and place, his world, his needs, and his personality. The story doesn't kick into gear, though, until you move from the skull to the spine, a connection known as the *inciting incident.*

We want to begin our story in the middle of the action, but this is not the same as the Big Incident. Save the big event for a few chapters later, after you've given us some time to know and understand your character's personality and his needs.

When I am teaching in front of a large group, I often engage a kindly conspirator to help me illustrate a point. As I talk about the skull of the plot skeleton, my conspirator will walk toward me and hand me a folded slip of paper. I open it, read it silently, then look out at the crowd and, with a woeful expression, tell them that Billy (or Jimmy or Paul or Elizabeth) has died.

The members of the audience give me sympathetic looks, but not until I say, "Excuse me—I meant Billy *Graham*" (or Jimmy Carter or Paul McCartney or Queen Elizabeth) do their faces register real shock and dismay.

The final effect depends upon what sort of crowd it is, but the difference in their reactions is remarkable. Why? Because they have memories of and feelings about Billy Graham or Paul McCartney or Queen Elizabeth. They don't have to be personally acquainted with Billy or Paul or the queen, but because they've heard about those people for years, there is a strong connection. And that's the sort of bond we want to develop in the first part of our novel. We want the reader to admire the protagonist, feel sympathy for him, like him, laugh with him, and root for him. We strive to build connection *before* the big story event takes place so the reader will truly care when the inciting incident occurs.

In the first 20 percent of *The Wizard of Oz* we learned that Dorothy loves Toto passionately and that Martha is a perfectionist chef. Yes, start in the middle of something active, but hold off on the big event for a while. Let us get to know your character first . . . because we won't gasp about their dilemma until we have thoroughly identified with them.

In a picture book, the inciting incident is often signaled by two words: "One day . . ." Those two words are a natural way to move from setting the stage to the action. As you plot your novel, ask yourself, "One day, what happens to move my main character into the action of the story?" Your answer will be your inciting incident, the key that turns your story engine.

After Dorothy runs away, if she'd made it home to Uncle Henry and Aunt Em without incident there would have been no story. But the inciting incident occurs: the tornado picks up Dorothy and drops her, along with her house, in the land of Oz.

Maria the postulant would have kept singing and not fitting in if not for the day Reverend Mother called her into her office and explained that the Von Trapp family needed a governess—and that Maria would be the perfect candidate.

A ringing telephone signals the inciting incident in *Mostly Martha*. When Martha takes the call, she learns that her sister, who was a single mother to an eight-year-old girl, has been killed in an auto accident.

Often—but not always—your protagonist doesn't want to go where the inciting incident pushes her. Obviously, Martha doesn't want to hear that her sister is dead, and she certainly doesn't want to be a mother. She takes Lina, her niece, and offers to cook for her (her way of showing love), but her effort is neither welcomed nor appreciated. Lina wants her mother, not gourmet food.

Maria the postulant is surprised to hear that the Reverend Mother wants to send her away from the convent, but she is guided by her faith in God and her obedience to her authority. So off she goes.

And Dorothy, of course, did not want to get picked up by a tornado, but she was helpless before the strong winds of Story. Like all protagonists, she found herself smack dab in the middle of the Story World, a place vastly different from the world she'd known before.

What is the inciting incident that pulls your protagonist out of his ordinary world and sets him on a different path? Is he set in motion by a letter or a summons?

I once heard a writer say that most stories commence when someone either comes to town or leaves town. That's not far from the truth—maybe your protagonist enters a special story world when someone comes to town and enters *his* world, thereby changing it.

Take a moment to jot down the situation that moves your protagonist from status quo to something new. Is it unique? Can you make it better?

Even if your protagonist has actively pursued a change, he or she may have moments of doubt as the entrance to the special world looms ahead. When your character retreats or doubts or refuses to leave the ordinary world, another character should step in to provide encouragement, advice, information, or a special tool. This will help your main character overcome those last-minute doubts and enable her to establish—

The End of the Spine: the Goal

At some point after the inciting incident, your character will establish and state a goal. Shortly after stepping out of her transplanted house, Dorothy looks around Oz and wails, "I want to go back to Kansas!" She's been transported over the rainbow, but she prefers the tried and true to the unfamiliar and strange. In order to go home, she'll have to visit the wizard in the Emerald City. As she tries to meet an ever-shifting set of subordinate goals (follow the yellow brick road, overcome the poppies, get in to see the wizard, bring back a broomstick), her main goal keeps viewers glued to the screen.

This overriding concern—will she or won't she make it home?—is sometimes called "the dramatic question." The dramatic question in every murder mystery is *Who committed the crime?* The dramatic question in nearly every thriller is *Who will win the inevitable showdown between the hero and the villain?* Along the way readers will worry about the subgoals (Will the villain kill his hostage? Will the hero figure out the clues?), but the dramatic question keeps them reading until the last page.

Maria's goal is simple: if God wants her to be a governess, she'll be the best governess she can be. But can she do that in Captain Von Trapp's unusual household?

Martha finds herself trying to care for a grieving eight-year-old who doesn't want another mother. So Martha promises to track down the girl's father, who lives in Italy. She knows only that his name is Giuseppe.

Make sure that your protagonist has an *observable* goal, one that would be filmable if you were making a movie. If her goal is simply to be a better person, how can that be measured? Instead, let your self-centered debutante decide to raise a million dollars for breast cancer research because it will help her get into Harvard, and then let us see how she becomes a more caring person on her quest to reach that goal.

Once your protagonist enters the special world, what goal does he set? Are there smaller tasks he must achieve in order to reach the ultimate goal? How will he measure his forward progress?

And ask yourself this—what happens if your character doesn't achieve his goal? If your answer is "life just returns to normal," you probably need to increase the risks your protagonist is taking. As he strives to reach his goal, he will need to mortgage the farm, burn a bridge, or walk away from a relationship. This undertaking can't be light or trivial; in order for it to mean a lot to the reader, it must mean a lot to the character.

After all, on her journey home Dorothy nearly loses Toto and her life to the witch. What is your character prepared to lose?

The Ribcage

Even my youngest students understand that a protagonist who accomplishes everything he attempts is a colorless character. As another friend of mine is fond of pointing out, when we tackle the mountain of life, it's the bumps we climb on!

If you're diagramming, sketch at least three curving ribs over your spine. These represent the *complications* that must arise to prevent your protagonist from reaching his goal.

Why at least three ribs? Because even in the shortest of stories—in a picture book, for instance—three complications works better than two or four. I don't know why three gives us such a feeling of completion, but it does.

While a very short story might have only three complications, a movie or novel may have hundreds. Complications can range from the mundane—John can't find a pencil to write down Sarah's number—to life-shattering. As you write down possible complications that could stand between your character and his ultimate goal, place the more serious problems at the bottom of the list.

The *stakes*—what your protagonist is risking—should increase in significance as the story progresses. In *Mostly Martha*, the complications center on this uptight woman's ability to care for a child. Lina hates her babysitter, so Martha has to take Lina to work with her. But the late hours take their toll, and Lina is habitually late for school. To pour salt in the wound, Lina keeps refusing to eat anything Martha cooks for her.

I asked you to make the ribs curve because any character that runs into complication after complication without any breathing space is going to be a weary character . . . and you'll weary your reader with this frenetic pace. One of the keys to good pacing is to alternate your plot complications with rewards. Like a pendulum that swings on an arc, let your character relax, if only briefly, between disasters.

Along the spiraling yellow brick road, Dorothy soon reaches an intersection (a complication). Fortunately, a friendly scarecrow is willing to help (a reward). They haven't gone far before Dorothy becomes hungry (a complication). The scarecrow spots an apple orchard ahead (a reward). These apple trees, however, resent being picked (a complication), but the clever scarecrow taunts them until they begin to throw fruit at the hungry travelers (a reward).

See how it works? Every negative complication is followed by a positive reward that matches the seriousness of the complication. Let's fast forward to the scene where the balloon takes off without Dorothy. This is a *severe* complication and it leads to *the bleakest moment*. Whether your story has had three or three hundred complications, the bleakest moment is the final rib in the ribcage, leading to the moment when your protagonist loses all hope.

In *The Sound of Music*, the complications are broader and slower-paced than in *The Wizard of Oz* which is, after all, a children's story. Who is the first person or group of people who stand between Maria and her goal of being the best governess she can be? That's right—the children themselves. They don't want a governess, and they pretty much tell her so when they are first introduced to her. The boys put a pinecone in her chair and a frog in her bed; they talk about how they got rid of their other governesses in no time flat. That's a complication.

But when a storm ensues, they run to Maria for comfort, and she allows them to snuggle with her while she sings them a song to make them forget their fears. And in no time at all, Maria has become one of their favorite things.

Who is the next person or persons who stand in the way of Maria's goal? The captain himself, of course. He has been (rather conveniently) away while Maria dealt with the complication of the children, but the highly disciplined widower arrives back home to find his children climbing trees in clothing made from curtains. He's horrified, and he blinks in astonishment after he announces that he will summon Maria by a certain whistle and she tells him that she doesn't *do* whistles, thank you very much. But he watches her even as they butt heads, and because she is warm and loving and truly cares for his children, she wins him over.

There's a third complication in Maria's story, and it does lead to a bleak moment. Who's the third person or persons who stand in Maria's way of being the best governess she can be? Most people immediately assume it's the Baroness, but it's not. Let me remind you of the pertinent scene:

The adults are all inside at the fancy dress ball to honor the Baroness, while Maria and the children are out on the patio. She's trying to teach them an Austrian folk dance, but Hans or Franz or whatever the oldest boy's name is can't seem to get the hang of it.

Suddenly Captain Von Trapp steps out onto the patio. With great dignity he says, "Allow me," and he takes Maria into his arms and they do the folk dance perfectly. When it's over, the captain returns to the ball and a flushed Maria turns to face the children.

Enter the Baroness. She sashays over to Maria and, ignoring the children, says, "You blushed in his arms just now," and Maria claps her hands to her burning face, then turns and runs . . . all the way back to the convent.

Let me ask again: who is the person who stands in the way of Maria's goal of being the best governess she can be? It's not the Baroness, though that lady did point out something crucial. The complication lies in Maria's own traitorous heart. She's in love with the captain, and how can a nun-in-training be a good governess if she's secretly in love with her employer?

She can't. And because Maria can't see any way out of her situation, she runs back to the convent, where she can tend to her broken heart in private. That is her bleakest moment.

So—what is the bleakest story in your existing plot? What has your character risked—and lost? A scholarship? The love of his life? His freedom? His reputation? His freedom?

If the situation he's facing isn't the worst complication he could face, or if there's an obvious way out of the problem, you need to rethink your plot. He needs to be at the end of his rope, and he should feel the pain of defeat. Your hero needs to be tested, as it were, through the fire in order to come out refined and strong.

Is your bleakest moment bleak enough? Has your protagonist truly found himself without hope?

The Thighbone: Send in the Cavalry

At the bleakest moment, your character needs *help*, but be careful how you deliver it. The ancient Greek playwrights had actors representing the Greek gods literally descend from a structure above in order to untangle their complicated plots and set things to rights. This sort of resolution is frowned upon in modern literature. Called *deus ex machina* (literally *god from the machine*), this device employs some unexpected and improbable incident to bring victory or success. If you find yourself whipping up a coincidence or a miracle after the bleakest moment, chances are you've employed deus ex machina. Back up and try again, please.

Avoid using deus ex machina by sending help, represented on the plot skeleton by the thigh bone. Your character obviously needs help; if he could solve the problem alone, he would have done it long before the bleakest moment. Having him conveniently remember something or stumble across a hidden resource smacks of coincidence and will leave your reader feeling resentful and cheated.

So send in the cavalry, but remember that *they can't solve the protagonist's problem*. They can give her a push in the right direction, they can nudge, they can remind, they can inspire. But they shouldn't wave a magic wand and make everything all right.

For Maria the nun-in-training, the Reverend Mother supplies the help she needs by reminding Maria that she shouldn't run from her problems, but find the courage to face them. And that she must "climb every mountain" until she finds her dream.

For Dorothy, help comes in the form of Glenda the Good Witch, who reveals a secret—the ruby slippers have the power to carry her back to Kansas. All Dorothy has to do is say "There's no place like home"—with feeling, mind you—and she'll be back on the farm with Uncle Henry and Auntie Em. Dorothy's problem isn't resolved, however, until she applies this information internally. At the beginning of the story, she wanted to be anywhere *but* on the farm. Now she has to affirm that the farm is where she wants to be. Her hidden need—to find a place to call home--has been met.

In *Mostly Martha*, the bleakest moment arrives with Lina's father, Giuseppe. He is a good man, and Lina seems to accept him. But after waving goodbye, Martha goes home to an empty apartment and realizes that she is not happy with her former childless life. She goes to Marlo, the Italian chef she has also begun to love, and asks for his help.

Who arrives to help your protagonist? To whom does she run for help? Does this person offer advice and a helping hand? Remember that the helper isn't meant to solve the problem, but to encourage and strengthen the protagonist until she realizes what she must do in order to reach her goal.

The Kneecap and Leg bone: A Lesson Leads to a Decision

Martha realizes that her old life was empty—she needs Lina, and she needs Marlo. So she and Marlo drive from Germany to Italy to fetch Lina and bring her home.

Draw a round kneecap and a shin bone—they represent the lesson learned and a decision to act. Both are important to story structure.

You may be hard pressed to cite the lesson you learned from the last novel you read, but your protagonist needs to learn something. This lesson is the *epiphany*, a sudden insight that speaks volumes to your character and brings them to the conclusion of their inner journey.

James Joyce popularized the word *epiphany*, literally *the manifestation of a divine being*. (Churches celebrate the festival of Epiphany on January sixth to commemorate the meeting of the Magi and the Christ child.) After receiving help from an outside source, your character should see something—a person, a situation, or an object—in a new light.

When the scarecrow asks why Glenda waited so long to explain the power of the ruby slippers, the good witch smiles and says, "Because she wouldn't have believed me. She had to learn it for herself."

The scarecrow then asks, "What'd you learn, Dorothy?"

Without hesitation, Dorothy announces that she's learned a lesson: "The next time I go looking for my heart's desire, I won't look any farther than my own back yard."

She has learned to appreciate her home, so even though she is surrounded by loving friends and a beautiful emerald city, Dorothy chooses to return to colorless Kansas. She hugs her friends once more, then grips Toto, clicks her heels, and *acts* upon what she's learned: home is where your loved ones are. Her hidden need, depicted at the beginning of the story, has been met.

Back in Austria, young Maria the postulant makes the decision to return to the Von Trapp family mansion in order to fulfill her promise to be a governess. The children are very happy to see her, and she tells the captain that she will remain as governess until he marries, then she'll leave.

And the captain says, "But I'm not marrying the Baroness . . . how could I, when I'm in love with someone else?"

And Maria learns that the captain loves her, and suddenly the family is planning a wedding.

The Sound of Music could have ended perfectly well at the wedding scene, but the film includes a few more scenes to explain how the Von Trapp family came to America to escape the Nazis. But the film is not a story about Nazis, it's a love story about the romance between a free-spirited postulant and a starched Navy captain. The movie is about love, not war, and at the end of the film we see that Maria's hidden need—to love and serve God and others—has been met many times over.

What does your protagonist learn in the course of his trial? What has he realized about his life, his past, or his future? Does he appreciate something or someone he used to take for granted? Write down what your character has learned, then show us how he can put this knowledge into action.

Armed with this new realization or understanding, what does your protagonist do that he could not do before? Does he go up against the villain with new strength or courage? Does he have a quality or a weapon he has suddenly begun to value? Does she humble herself for the first time, or confess something she would never have confessed before? What can your protagonist do to show the reader that he or she has truly experienced a deep and personal shift in attitude?

The Foot: The Resolution

Every story needs the fairy-tale equivalent of "and they lived happily ever after" as the protagonist leaves the story world and returns to his ordinary world a changed person. Not every story ends happily, of course, though happy endings are undoubtedly the most popular. Some protagonists are sadder and wiser after the course of their adventure. But even if a protagonist does not get what he worked for, a novel should leave the reader with hope.

The resolution to *Mostly Martha* is portrayed during the closing of the film. As the credits roll, we see Marlo and Martha meeting

Lina in Italy, we see Martha in a wedding gown (with her hair down!) and Marlo in a tuxedo, we see a wedding feast with Giuseppe, his family, and Martha's German friends, we see Martha and Marlo and Lina exploring an abandoned restaurant—clearly, they are going to settle in Italy so Lina can be a part of both families. In the delightful final scene, we again see Martha with her therapist, but this time he has cooked for *her* and she is counseling him.

Many movies end with a simple visual image—we see a couple walking away hand-in-hand, a mother cradling her long-lost son. That's all we need to realize that our main character has struggled, learned, and come away a better (or wiser) person. As a writer, you'll have to use words instead of images, but you can paint the same sort of reassuring picture without resorting to "and they lived happily ever after."

Your story should end with a changed protagonist—he or she has gone through a profound experience and has changed as a result, hopefully for the better. Your protagonist has completed an outer journey (experienced the major plot events) and an inner journey that addressed some hurt from the past and resulted in a changed character. When he reenters his ordinary world, he has a new understanding or circumstance to share with others.

What scenes can you depict that show us that your character has changed permanently? Is a wedding appropriate? A change of career? A change of scenery? Come up with a simple scene or two that lets the reader know that life is going to be different for your protagonist from this point on.

Does Every Character Need a Skeleton?

Yes and no. I usually sketch out brief plot skeletons for all the major characters if only to remind myself that they need goals and a reason for being in the story. If your secondary characters are only hanging around to interact with the protagonist at appropriate times, they'll be as thin as an insincere smile. You don't have to create their plot skeletons all the way down to the thighbone, but they should have histories and goals.

Remember the Scarecrow, the Tin Man, and the Cowardly Lion? These secondary characters in *The Wizard of Oz* had histories (far more developed in the book than in the film), and they spent a lot of time pursuing personal goals while at Dorothy's side. We cheered for them when they received something better than a brain, a heart, and courage. They received the recognition that they had already proved themselves intelligent, loving, and brave friends to our heroine from Kansas.

So give your secondary characters a full life, and use the plot skeleton to pinpoint their highlights. Give them goals, and weave their pursuits along with the protagonist's. You never know what unexpected developments might occur when the two storylines intersect.

Is That All There is to It?

Depends. You have probably heard that some stories are more plot-driven or character-driven, and that's true. Let's leave the skeleton for a moment and focus on a circle. Let's say that the right side of the circle represents the plot action while the left side of the circle represents character growth.

 In some action movies—the James Bond franchise comes to mind—nearly all the story is contained on the right side of the circle. James changes very little as a person, and we learn very little about him. (I've been pleased to see that we are beginning to learn about James in the more recent Bond films—maybe we'll have some real character development in the future!)

James is focused on saving the world from evil henchmen, and when that's done, he seems to care only about the beautiful woman he met in the course of his adventure.

On the other hand, in other stories the emphasis is on the character side of the circle. In my book *The Fine Art of Insincerity*, three sisters gather together over Labor Day weekend to clean out their late grandmother's beach house. That's about all the action there is.

But while the sisters are together, the oldest woman learns that her husband has been unfaithful and that her youngest sister was planning to commit suicide on the drive home—earth-shattering revelations that rock her world. The sisters come together to confront, accuse, confess, and reconcile all the traumatic events of their shared past.

A character driven story still needs a plot—you need something to get the characters together and move them around—but most of the emotion is invested in what the characters are feeling and how they're reacting to one another. They're not out to save the world, find romance, or win a prize; they are out to restore faded relationships or establish new ones.

An acquaintance once told me that character-driven stories always win the Oscar for Best Picture at the Academy Awards. *Driving Miss Daisy* and *Steel Magnolias* are prime examples of character stories. They can make me cry just by talking about them.

Let's look first at *Driving Miss Daisy*. Daisy Werthan is the protagonist, and she has an obvious problem at the opening of the story—she needs a driver, because she's aging and her son insists that she's no longer safe behind the wheel. Ms. Daisy has a hidden need, too, one that no one sees: she is a prejudiced product of her generation.

So Daisy, grumbling the entire time, soon receives Hoke, a black chauffeur. A great distance exists between Daisy and her driver, illustrated at mealtimes: Daisy eats alone in the dining room, while Hoke eats in the kitchen with Idella the cook. The kitchen is filled with laughter and warmth; Daisy remains alone in the chilly silence.

After a while, Daisy asks Hoke to drive her to Alabama. He does, but on the long journey, he asks permission to stop the car so he can "make water." He is clearly uncomfortable to have to ask, and Daisy is horrified at the request and refuses to allow him to stop. But Hoke, driven by physical necessity, finally stops, and we realize that Daisy could not even admit that Hoke was a man, with a man's need to relieve himself.

Later, Daisy's synagogue is bombed, and she is terribly shaken that anyone could be so evil and prejudiced. How could such things happen? She cannot see that in her own way, she is as prejudiced as those who hate Jews.

When Martin Luther King Jr. comes to town for a dinner, Daisy plans to give her extra ticket to her son Booley, but he has to back out at the last moment. So Daisy sits next to an empty chair at the banquet, a seat that could and should have gone to Hoke, but Daisy can't even imagine the idea of a black driver sitting next to her at such an important banquet. Hoke has to listen to Dr. King's speech on a car radio in the parking lot.

But in Daisy's bleakest moment, when her dementia worsens

and she wakes up one morning thinking that she's a schoolteacher once again, it's Hoke who calms her and cares for her and calls her son.

And at the end of the film, when Daisy is in a nursing home, it's Hoke who comes to visit her. She looks at him, smiles, and says, with deep feeling, "You're my best friend."

And he is.

Daisy has come a long way in that character arc, and that's where the true heart of the story lies. *Driving Miss Daisy* isn't about a woman's need for a driver. It's about the friendship that develops between a white Jewish woman and a black man.

In *Steel Magnolias*, M'Lynn is the protagonist, even though she's surrounded by a stellar supporting cast who play colorful strong characters. M'Lynn's obvious problem is that her daughter's getting married and everything's hectic, but goal soon becomes obvious: Shelby, her daughter, has severe diabetes, and M'Lynn is determined to nag, scold, remind, and do anything she has to do in order to protect her daughter's life and health.

But Shelby cares more about living than being protected, and though she and her mother are constantly butting heads, Shelby prevails. She marries her sweetheart, has a baby, survives a kidney transplant, and then, tragically, her body gives out and she dies.

M'Lynn doesn't achieve her goal, and she is devastated. But through the care and support of her friends, she learns that life goes on. She has Shelby's son to live for, and the future beckons even though she will always grieve for the daughter she lost.

Yes, there's a plot—M'Lynn is always trying to protect Shelby. But the true heart of the story is about how women support and care for one another.

How can you tell if a story is more character- or plot driven? Try to describe the story to a friend. If you say, "This is about a boy and his dog as they try to win an Alaskan race," then clearly it's plot-driven. But if you find yourself saying, "This is about a boy and how he becomes a man through loving and caring for his sled dog," then you're apt to be describing a character story.

Stories should have both plot and character arcs, and they may be evenly balanced. Events move the story along and characters grow and change as the story progresses. But the balance between plot and character can shift from one side to the other without changing the quality of the story. One emphasis is not better than the other because the balance will depend upon the sort of story you want to tell.

Write what is best-suited for the story you have in mind. You will tell it unlike anyone else.

Brandon takes a Bath

While I would love to take one of my novel manuscripts and point out exactly the bones of the plot skeleton fit into the story, I can't squeeze all those words into this little book. So to illustrate how simple plotting by skeleton is, let me present the script to one of my picture books. Picture books are spare by design, with a limited number of words, and often some of the plot elements are implied. But I think it should be easy to see how it all comes together in even a simple little story like this one.

I've put my plot comments in brackets and bold type.

The opening: the protagonist's (Brandon's) ordinary world:

Yesterday I spent the day at my cousins' house. Aunt Molly, Uncle George, and my cousins Sam and Tricia are calm, quiet people, but Brandon is something else.

Brandon played outside in the mud and wrote on himself with colored markers. At dinner, he put spaghetti on his head. It was a messy, dirty day. [**Obvious need: a bath. Hidden need: like all little kids, Brandon needs to know he's loved.**]

After supper Aunt Molly asked, "Brandon, are you ready to take a bath?" [**The inciting incident: Mom's invitation.**]
Brandon shook his head. "No," he said. "I'm not ready to take a bath." [**Brandon's goal: avoid the bath! Bathtime signals an end to the day, an end to his fun.**]

[**We move into the Story World: the bathroom.**]
"But Brandon," Uncle George said, "if you take a bath you will be clean and sweet-smelling." [**He's urging Brandon toward the tub.**]
Brandon made fish faces at Tricia. "I'm not ready to take a bath." [**Brandon counters by doing something else. This pattern will be repeated many times.**]

"Brandon," Aunt Molly said, "I'm giving the bath water a squirt of bubbling super soap. You can soak in mountains of bubbles."
Brandon twirled on his toes and said, "I'm not ready to take a bath."

"Brandon," Sam said, "I'm putting my toy boat in the tub. You can sail it."
Brandon stood on his head and said, "I'm not ready to take a bath."

"Brandon," Tricia said, "I'm putting toy dishes in the tub. You can pretend to pour milk and coffee."
Brandon somersaulted across the floor. "I'm not ready to take a bath."

"Brandon," Aunt Molly called, "I'm putting your beach bucket and shovel in the tub. You can scoop up bubbles and put them in the bucket."
Brandon marched like a soldier and said, "I'm-not-rea-dy-to-take-a-bath."

"Brandon," called Uncle George, "I'm blowing up your swimming ring seahorse for the tub."
Brandon started pulling the laces out of his dad's sneakers. "I'm not ready to take a bath."

"Brandon," Sam said, "I'm putting Howard in the water. You can swim with your pet turtle."
Brandon found the day-old lollipop he'd stuck under the table. "I'm not ready to take a bath."

"Brandon," I said, holding up a bottle from the kitchen, "I'm squirting green drops in your bath water. You can play in colored bubbles!"
Brandon hopped like a rabbit and squeaked. "I'm not ready to take a bath."

Uncle George sighed and turned to Aunt Molly. "I suppose we could skip bathtime and move straight to bedtime. Because

Brandon simply doesn't want to take a bath." **[The opposition closes in, leading to Brandon's bleakest moment—though, admittedly, in this children's story it's not terribly bleak.]**
"*Now* I do," Brandon shouted. "But there's no room for me in the tub!" **[Cornered, Brandon takes the most favorable option.]**

"No problem," said Uncle George. "We'll make room."
Uncle George took out the seahorse.
Aunt Molly took out the bucket and shovel.
Sam took out the turtle and the boat.
Tricia took out the toy dishes.
But I *couldn't* take the green drops out of the water. **[The unseen narrator acts as helper. She has inadvertently provided Brandon with a means of escape.]**

Brandon took off his dirty clothes and climbed in the tub. He splashed and played, and played and splashed. Finally he called, "I'm ready to get out!"

"Oh no!" Aunt Molly said, peeking in at him. "He's green!"
"Brandon," said Uncle George, "Wouldn't you like to take a nice, clean bath?"

Brandon shook his green hair and climbed out of the tub. "Not now. I'm not ready to take a bath!" **[Resolution: Brandon runs out of the bathroom, heading back to his ordinary world of play and fun with two easy-going parents and siblings.]**

Learning to Spot the Bones
Now that you've learned what the elements of plot structure are, be alert for them. Because screenplays are so tightly-formatted due to time constraints, the inciting incident usually falls somewhere around 20-25 minutes into the movie. My husband is accustomed to me looking at my watch and saying, "Something big is about to happen right . . . now."

So as you watch movies and read books, take notes and see if you can pinpoint the moments when the character establishes a goal, faces a new complication, and experiences a bleakest moment. Who comes to help him? What decision does he make after that? What does he learn about himself? How does he change over the course of the story? And what can he do at the end of the story that he could not do at the beginning? That action or attitude is evidence that his hidden need—his wound from the past—is healing.

Learning how to identify the bones of plot structure will help you plot your own stories more easily. And once you have sketched out the bones of your own story, you don't have to pull out your hair over writing a synopsis—just turn your plot skeleton into brief paragraphs and you're done. You have a beginning, a middle, and an end. You have everything you need to put into a proposal for a novel or to start crafting that screenplay. Or, if you're writing something shorter, you have everything you need to start working.

Now you're ready to begin writing scenes. Tape your synopsis to your desk, take a deep breath, and plunge ahead. Don't forget your plot skeleton—keep it in view and refer to it often.

Whenever I have found myself bogged down in a story and unsure of where to turn next, it's invariably because I've gone down a rabbit trail or somehow become unfocused. Whenever that happens, I pull out my plot skeleton and remind myself of what it is my characters are working toward. What is their hidden need, and how are they changing so that it will be met? What is their goal, and how do their current activities either push them toward their goal or distract them from it?

With a little reminder from my scrawny plot skeleton, I am back on my way within minutes.

Now it's your turn. Go write something wonderful.

Book 2 in the *Lesson from the Writing Front* series, *Know Your Characters*, will be available in July 2013.

ABOUT THE AUTHOR

Angela Hunt writes for readers who have learned to expect the unexpected from this versatile writer. With over four million copies of her books sold worldwide, she is the best-selling author of more than 120 works ranging from picture books (*The Tale of Three Trees*) to novels and nonfiction.

Now that her two children have reached their twenties, Angie and her husband live in Florida with Very Big Dogs (a direct result of watching *Turner and Hooch* too many times). This affinity for mastiffs has not been without its rewards—one of their dogs was featured on *Live with Regis and Kelly* as the second-largest canine in America. Their dog received this dubious honor after an all-expenses-paid trip to Manhattan for the dog and the Hunts, complete with VIP air travel and a stretch limo in which they toured New York City. Afterward, the dog gave out pawtographs at the airport.

Angela admits to being fascinated by animals, medicine, unexplained phenomena, and "just about everything." Books, she says, have always shaped her life— in the fifth grade she learned how to flirt from reading *Gone with the Wind*.

Her books have won the coveted Christy Award, several Angel Awards from Excellence in Media, and the Gold and Silver Medallions from *Foreword Magazine*'s Book of the Year Award. In 2007, her novel *The Note* was featured as a Christmas movie on the Hallmark channel. She recently completed her doctorate in biblical literature and is now finishing her doctorate in Theology.

When she's not home writing, Angie often travels to teach writing workshops at schools and writers' conferences. And to talk about her dogs, of course. Readers may visit her web site at www.angelahuntbooks.com.

Selected Books by Angela Hunt

The Offering
The Fine Art of Insincerity
Five Miles South of Peculiar
The Face
Let Darkness Come
The Elevator
The Novelist
The Awakening
The Truth Teller
Unspoken
Uncharted
The Justice
The Canopy
The Immortal
Doesn't She Look Natural ?
She Always Wore Red
She's In a Better Place
The Pearl
The Note
The Debt
Then Comes Marriage
The Shadow Women
Dreamers
Brothers
Journey
Roanoke
Jamestown
Hartford
Rehoboth
Charles Towne
The Proposal
The Silver Sword
The Golden Cross
The Velvet Shadow
The Emerald Isle

Made in the USA
Lexington, KY
03 July 2013